ALLEN J. WOPPERT

The Case of the Corner Shop Robbers

CORNELSEN
ENGLISH
LIBRARY

Cornelsen

CORNELSEN **ENGLISH** LIBRARY
Allen J. Woppert · The Case of the Corner Shop Robbers

Verlagsredaktion
Julie Colthorpe

Umschlaggestaltung
havemannundmosch, Konzeption und Gestaltung, Berlin

Titelbild
Rob Cousins

Illustration
Fliss Cary

Gestaltung & technische Umsetzung
Anna Bakalović und Annika Preyhs, Berlin

www.cornelsen.de

1. Auflage, 9. Druck 2021

Alle Drucke dieser Auflage sind inhaltlich unverändert
und können im Unterricht nebeneinander verwendet werden.

Druck: AZ Druck und Datentechnik GmbH, Kempten

ISBN 978-3-06-031211-5

Contents

....

Chapter 1   Goodbye school, hello summer!

....

"... So have a great summer, all of you" Mr Kingsley said. "I'm planning to have a fantastic summer without you."

The kids of 7PK all laughed. It was the last day of school, and everybody was happy. Mr Kingsley, their form teacher,
5   went on.

"Please be careful, everybody. I want to see all of you in six weeks!"

The students clapped and started to put their things in their school bags.

10   "Did Mr Kingsley look at us when he said, 'Be careful'?" Jack asked.

"Yes, I think he did," answered Sophie. The group started to go.

"Well, I can understand that!" Ananda said. "After what
15 happened with Mr Green and the man in black."

"Yes, Jack," Jo said. "You and Sophie are heroes. The police said so."

"No," Jack said. "We're all heroes. We're the SHoCK Team."

20   "S for Shaw," Jo said.

"H for Hanson," Jack said.

"C for Carter-Brown," said Sophie.

"K for Kapoor," said Ananda.

The friends all laughed – but not Dan. He didn't look
25 happy.

"You're very quiet, little brother," Jo said. "What's wrong?" He liked to call Dan "little brother". Jo was born 20 minutes before his twin brother, and Dan didn't like the name. But today Dan didn't want to argue.

"Nothing's wrong," he answered.

"But?" Sophie asked.

Dan didn't want to answer. But his friends waited. He had to say something. "Well, it's just … six weeks without you all …"

"Oh, that's so sweet," Ananda said.

"We can meet in the summer, Dan," Sophie added.

"Yeah," said Jack. "And we can talk on the phone."

"And write text messages," added Jo.

"That's right," Ananda said. "And when I go to New York, I can send you a postcard."

"New York?!" everybody said. "You didn't tell us that!"

"Dilip and I are going to New York to visit our aunt and uncle and cousin. I didn't want to tell you about it because I wasn't sure. The tickets came yesterday."

"Wow," said Sophie. "New York! My parents are just planning to take us to Majorca."

"Just?" said Jo. "We're planning to go to Cornwall with our dad this year. But it's very expensive."

"What about me?" Jack asked. "We never go away in the summer. We can't. It's the best time of year for the B & B."

"Poor Jack!" said Sophie, and everybody agreed.

They were outside the school now, and they were all very quiet. They didn't know what to say. After a time, Dan said, "See you all soon then."

And they all went home.

Chapter 2   Holidays can be boring

The first week, Dan and Jo thought the holidays were great. It wasn't too hot and it was never cold or rainy.

On the first day the twins went to the swimming pool. On the second day they played some football. On the third day
5 Jo went to the Downs for more football, and Dan sat in the garden and read a book. On the fourth day their dad took them to ride go-karts.

"Why can't we always have holidays?" Jo said and sat down in his go-kart.

10 Dan looked at him. "Because you can't always be stupid, Jo," he answered.

Jo wanted to say something, but Dan was already on his go-kart and far away. "Come back here!" Jo shouted and started his go-kart.

15 Mr Shaw just laughed and started his go-kart. "The loser has to buy the ice creams!" he shouted.

Later all three sat at the ice cream place – Mr Shaw bought the ice creams. "So, you two," he started, "are you having good holidays?"

20 "Yes, Dad," both boys answered.

"Great!" Jo added.

"That's good," Mr Shaw said. "Because I remember, when I was 12 …"

"You had to walk ten miles to school?" Jo asked.

25 "Wasn't it twenty?" Dan added. "In the wind and rain?"

"Ha, ha, Dan and Jo," their father said. "That's very funny. I wanted to say that I remember: holidays can be boring."

"No, Dad," Jo said. "Never!"

"Everything is cool, Dad," said Dan. "Don't worry."

Two days later, Dan and Jo were at the swimming pool again. It was nice and hot, there were lots of people to play football with, but …

"This is boring," Jo said.

5 "Yeah," said Dan.

"I think I miss school," Jo said. Then he added, "And don't tell our friends I said that!"

"I miss our friends," Dan said. "Let's call them."

"Yeah," Jo said. "Maybe tomorrow."

10 At the Pretty Polly Bed and Breakfast, Jack helped his parents every day of the first week. There were guests in all the rooms, and most were only there for two days. Mrs Hanson went to work every day, so Jack and his dad had a lot of work.

15 Jack usually finished his jobs before 12.30 or 1 o'clock, but then he was tired. Sometimes he sat at his computer and wrote stories. They were stories about spies and bank robbers. And sometimes they were stories about his friends in the SHoCK Team.

20 "I miss my friends," he said to his computer. But the computer didn't answer.

Ding-dong. The doorbell. "Can you go to the door, Jack?" his dad shouted from the bathroom.

"OK, Dad," he answered and ran downstairs. It was
25 the new guests, from Germany. "Guten Tag," Jack said. "Welcome to the Pretty Polly."

"Pretty Polly! Pretty Polly!" said Polly the parrot from the kitchen.

"Ach, jetzt verstehe ich," said the German woman. "Now
30 I know why you are the Pretty Polly B & B."

Jack helped the new guests to take their bags to their room. Then he went back upstairs to his computer.

"I miss my friends," he said again. "Maybe I can call them tomorrow."

5 At the Carter-Browns' house, Sophie wasn't happy. After a week of summer holidays, she was bored.

"I miss my friends," she told Prunella.

"I'm your friend," Prunella said.

"Yes, you are, Prunella," Sophie said. "But you're a
10 poltergeist. I miss my real friends – at school."

"I'm real," Prunella said. She didn't sound happy.

"Yes, I know, Prunella. I'm sorry."

"I've got an idea," Prunella said. "Maybe we can play games here."

15 "Like what?" Sophie asked.

"Well, we can go to your sister's room and throw her things out of the window."

"I can't do that, Prunella," Sophie said. "I don't want problems with Emily. And anyway that's a poltergeist
20 game."

"Hmm, maybe we can go to your parents' room and drop things."

"That's a poltergeist game too, Prunella."

"We can open and close things," Prunella said. "That's
25 always fun."

"Poltergeist."

"Oh, I know!" Prunella said. "We can … – er, no. That's for poltergeists too."

"Poor me," Sophie said.

30 "Why don't you just call your friends?" Prunella asked.

"I can't do that, Prunella. Oh, I can just hear Jo Shaw: 'Sophie Carter-Brown has got a boring life. She doesn't know how to have fun.' No, I can't call them."

"Real people are so difficult!" Prunella said. And then she went away.

At 13 Paul Road, Mr and Mrs Kapoor and their son Dilip were at work in their corner shop.

"Dilip!" Mrs Kapoor called. "Can you bring me that big box, please? The box of toilet paper?"

"I can do it," Ananda said.

"Ananda," her mother said. "I didn't hear you come down. I thought you were still in bed."

"No, Mum," she answered. "I wanted to help down here in the shop."

"No, no, Ananda dear," her mum said. "It's your holidays. You can't work."

"It's my holidays too, Mum," Dilip said. "Why do I have to work?"

Just then Mr Kapoor came in. "Because you're older, Dilip," he said. "And you're a boy."

"What do you mean, Ravi," asked Mrs Kapoor, "when you say, 'because he's a boy'? I'm a woman, and I work a lot!"

"I know, Meera, I know," Mr Kapoor answered. "I only wanted …"

Dilip looked at Ananda, and Ananda looked at Dilip. "Let's go to the café and have an ice cream," Dilip suggested. "This is boring."

"Very," Ananda said. "I miss my friends."

"Why don't you call them?" Dilip asked when they sat down outside the café.

"Oh, I'm sure they're all doing exciting things," she said. "And in two weeks …"

"New York!"

"Till then," Ananda said, "boring!"

Chapter 3 The first robberies

....

The next morning, Ananda and her parents were in the kitchen. Dilip was downstairs in the shop.

Mrs Kapoor was at the cooker. "I like it when you're home on holiday. I can make you breakfast."

5 Ananda laughed. "Yes, and my jeans don't fit! I can't eat like this every day, Mum."

"Oh, it isn't so much," Mrs Kapoor said. She put down a big plate of breakfast in front of Ananda. "I want to do something for my little girl before she goes to New York."

10 "Quiet, please," Mr Kapoor said. "I'd like to hear this."

It was something on the radio: "... and the police say they still don't know who the robbers are. Again, this was the fifth robbery at a corner shop in Bristol in the last two weeks. – This is Cliff Whittaker for Radio Bristol."

15 Mr Kapoor turned off the radio. It was very quiet in the kitchen for a minute. All three jumped when they heard the phone.

"Hello?" Mrs Kapoor said. "Yes, Mrs Khan, we heard it too. ... Yes, it's terrible. ... I agree, Mrs Khan. ... Yes, that's
20 a very good idea. ... Please tell me when it is. ... Thank you, Mrs Khan. ... Goodbye."

"That was Mrs Khan," Mrs Kapoor said to Ananda and Mr Kapoor. "She wants a meeting – all the corner shop owners and the police."

25 "How can a meeting help, Mum?" Ananda asked. She sounded afraid.

"I don't know, dear," Mrs Kapoor answered.

"I know one thing," Mr Kapoor said. "Dilip can't work in the shop now. And you can't be in the shop. Not till the police find those robbers."

"But Dad," Ananda said.

5   "No, dear, your dad is right," her mum said. "You and Dilip stay away from the shop. It's too dangerous."

Mr Kapoor got up from his chair.

"Where are you going, Ravi?" Mrs Kapoor asked.

"Downstairs to the shop, Meera," he answered. "Dilip is
10 there alone."

The meeting of the corner shop owners with the police was that evening. Mr Kapoor stayed in the shop. Ananda went with her mother to the meeting. Dilip went to a disco.

"There are lots of people here!" Ananda said.

5 "Yes, there are. I didn't know there were so many corner shops in Bristol."

There weren't enough chairs for everybody, so Ananda went to the back. Suddenly she heard a voice. "Ananda."

It was Pak Lee, a Korean boy from school. "Oh, hi," she
10 said.

"I didn't know your parents had a corner shop," Pak said.

"And I didn't know your parents had one."

"Oh yes, not far from school. We were the first."

15 "The first corner shop in Bristol?" Ananda asked.

"No," he laughed. "The robbers came to our shop first. That was two weeks ago."

"How terrible," Ananda said. "Were you there?"

"No, my mum. Now she can't sleep at night. She has bad
20 dreams all the time."

"I'm so sorry," Ananda said. "My mum and dad are really scared. Now my brother and I can't …"

Someone at the front of the room started to talk, so Ananda and Pak were quiet. They listened to the victims of
25 the first five robberies. Pak's mum was the first.

"There were three boys, maybe 17 or 18 years old," she said. "They had baseball bats, all three. And they had dark blue sweatshirts – hoodies. I didn't really see their faces."

Then the other victims told their stories: Three young
30 men. Blue hoodies. Baseball bats. They come in and shout, "Go into the back room!" They take money and cigarettes and leave.

Then a policeman went to the front. But the corner shop owners didn't like what he said.

"I'm afraid we can't do very much for you," he told them.

5   "The police are never there when you need them," shouted a man.

"Wait, wait, please," said the policeman. "I only wanted to say that we can't have somebody outside every corner shop."

10   The people were quiet again.

"Our cars can go past your shops more. We can try and visit corner shops more. But we can't be there all the time.

"Please don't be afraid to call us. If you see something funny, call us. Don't wait for a robbery. We can be there in
15 two or three minutes, so please call us."

The meeting went on for another hour, but there was nothing new. Ananda thought: "I have to do something. But what?"

Then she remembered: "The SHoCK Team!"

Chapter 4   Detective work

The others were very happy when Ananda called. They met the next day at the Pretty Polly B & B, in Jack's room.

"This is great," Jack said. "A new case for the SHoCK Team!"

5   "Yeah," said Jo. "We can be heroes again."

But Dan said, "Ananda and her family are very scared. Don't be so happy."

"Thanks, Dan," Ananda said. "It really is very scary. So I hope we can do something."

10   "We can watch the shop," said Sophie, "and …"

"And when the robbers come," Jo said, "we …"

"If the robbers come," Dan corrected.

"Right," said Jo. "If the robbers come, we can fight them. Wham! Pow! Whoop!"

15   "Jo," Ananda said, "the robbers are 17 or 18 years old."

"And big and strong," Jack added.

"And they've got baseball bats," said Dan.

"Oh," said Jo, "right."

"I wanted to say," said Sophie as she looked at Jo, "we
20   can watch the shop, and if the robbers come, we can call the police."

"Maybe we can do more," Jack said.

"But how?" Dan asked.

"I know," Jo said.

25   "You?" Ananda asked.

"Well, I can try," said Jo. "What do we know about the robberies?"

"I've got my notes from the meeting," Ananda said.

"Jack," said Jo, "have you got a map of Bristol?"

"Lots of them," Jack answered. "We give them to the guests at the B & B."

"Great," said Jo. "Can you get me one?"

"Sure," said Jack, and he ran downstairs to get a map.

5 "Jo," said Dan, "is this another one of your stupid ideas?"

"Just wait and see, little brother."

Jack came back with some maps. "Here you are, Jo."

"Now, where was the first robbery, Ananda?" Jo asked.

10 Ananda looked at her notes. "Let me see, … ah, here it is. The first robbery was on the corner of Alma Road and Alexandra Road."

Jo marked the place on one of the maps. "And when was it?"

15 "Two weeks ago," Ananda said. "It was on Thursday at 5.15 in the afternoon."

Jo wrote the time next to the place on the map. "And the second robbery?"

They did the same thing for all five robberies. Now the 20 map had five marks and some words on it. The five friends all looked at the map for a minute. Dan was the first to say something. "That didn't help us."

"No, I can't see a pattern," said Sophie.

"But the police on TV always do that," Jo said.

25 "This isn't TV, Jo," Dan said. He took the map and looked again. "No, there's no pattern. We can throw this away."

"Wait!" Jack said. "I have an idea. Give me the map."

Dan gave Jack the map. Then Jack opened a cupboard and started to look for something.

30 "What are you doing, Jack?" asked Sophie.

"I'm looking for my … ah, here it is!" Jack showed them his compass.

"You want to draw circles?" Dan asked.

"Are you mad, Jack?" Jo said.

"I don't under… oh, yes I do!" said Ananda. "That's a great idea!"

5   Jo looked at Sophie, Sophie looked at Dan and Dan looked at Jo. "Now they're both mad," Jo said.

Jack and Ananda went to Jack's desk and started to work on the map. Jack drew circles in different colours, and Ananda did some maths. The others just looked. A few
10 minutes later, Jack shouted, "I've got it!"

"You've got what?" Sophie asked.

Ananda explained. "Well, Jo had the right idea with the map."

"I did?" said Jo.

"Yes, but you have to do more."

"That's why I got my compass," said Jack.

"It's very easy really," Ananda said. "I can explain."

5 "Yes, please," said Sophie. She sat down on Jack's bed next to the twins.

Jack started. "In the city, a person walks about three miles in an hour."

"That's this much on the map," Ananda said. She showed
10 them Jack's compass – it was open 12 centimetres.

"That's one and a half miles in half an hour," Jack went on.

"Or this much on the map." Ananda showed them the compass again – it was open six centimetres.

15 "Right," said Dan. "I understand."

"Me too," said Sophie.

"I understand too," Jo said. "But we don't know where the robbers started."

"That's why I needed the compass," Jack explained. "All
20 the robberies were on Mondays and Thursdays in the early evening. So maybe the robbers started at the same time on those days."

"And in the same place," Ananda added.

"But we don't know when and we don't know where,"
25 Dan said.

"Do you remember what we learned about 'Trial and Error' in Science class?" Ananda asked.

"Of course," said Dan. "You guess something, and then you try it. It usually isn't right, so you guess again and try
30 that. You do that again and again till your guess is right."

"Yes," Jack said. "So we guessed that the robbers started at 5 o'clock. Ananda did the maths for each robbery: how far did the robbers walk from 5 o'clock to a robbery at 5.15?"

"Let's see ...," Sophie answered. "Three quarters of a mile."

"Right," Jack went on. "So I drew a circle for three quarters of a mile from the first robbery. The second robbery was at 5.05, so I drew another circle for that. Then I did the same for the third, fourth and fifth robberies."

"And?" Dan asked. "What did you find?"

"Nothing," said Ananda. "The robbers didn't start at 5 o'clock."

"All that for nothing?" Jo asked.

"Remember, Jo: Trial and Error," Jack said. "We tried 4.45 next, then 4.30, and then ..." Jack showed his friends the last map. "The robbers started at 4.35 from the corner of Walton Street and Chaplin Road!"

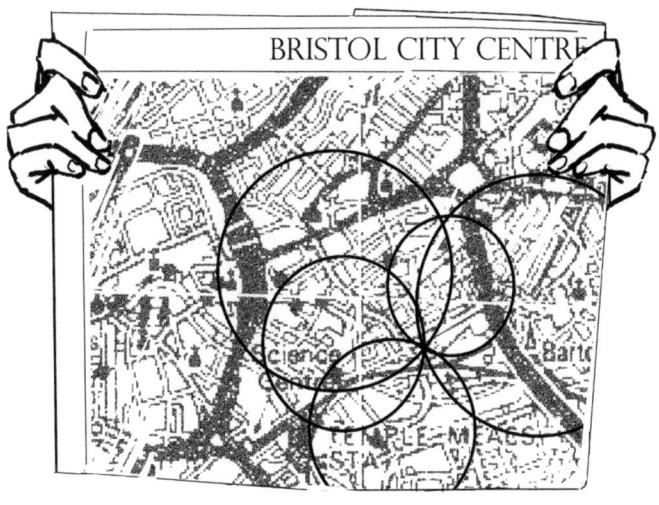

"Hey, you two," Sophie said, "that's fantastic!"

"Yeah," said Dan, "that's really great!"

And Jo said, "I don't really understand what you did. But I'm happy that we now know where to start."

5   "Well," said Ananda, "the next robbery isn't till Monday. So what do we do now?"

"How about an ice cream?" Jack said. "There's a good place for ice cream near here."

"Sounds good," they all agreed.

10   "We can talk about who does what at the ice cream place," Sophie said. And off they went.

Chapter 5   Hoodies, hoodies everywhere

The next Monday afternoon, at 4.15, the SHoCK Team were all in their places. Ananda and Sophie were on the street corner opposite the Kapoors' shop. Jack, Dan and Jo were in St Paul's, at the corner of Walton Street and Chaplin Road.

5   "I don't see any blue hoodies," Jo said.

"Give them time," Jack said. "It's early."

"And remember, Jo," said Dan. "If we see them, …"

"I know, I know," said Jo. "We follow them – nothing more."

10   The three boys waited and waited. Then, at 4.30, Dan whispered, "Don't look. Three blue hoodies on my left."

"Where?" said Jo. He turned around to look.

"I said, 'Don't look', Jo!" whispered Dan.

"They can't see us, Dan," said Jo. "They're still far
15   away."

The two brothers started to argue. Now Jack turned to look. "Hey, you two, I can't see them," he said.

"What?!" both twins said. They looked. Jack was right. There were no boys with blue hoodies on the street.

20   "They were there a minute ago," Dan said.

"Yes, I saw them too," said Jo.

"Maybe they went into one of the houses," Jack said.

Just then two boys in blue hoodies came round the corner. "Only two now," Dan said.

25   "No, six," said Jo. Four more boys in blue hoodies came round the corner.

"Seven," said Dan.

"Nine," said Jack.

"Where are they all coming from?" Dan asked.

"I don't know," answered Jack. "Let's go and look."

The boys started to walk to the next corner. They were scared: if they were right, three of the boys in hoodies were dangerous robbers!

5 When Jack, Dan and Jo got to the next corner, the street was empty. They walked down the street where the boys in blue sweatshirts came from. Then they heard someone shout. "See you on Thursday, Bob!"

The boys turned to look. A boy in a blue hoodie was in 10 front of an old church. He took his bike and started to walk down the street. The boy didn't look dangerous, so Jo talked to him.

"Excuse me," Jo said.

Dan and Jack were very afraid, but the boy just looked at 15 Jo and said, "Yes, can I help you?"

"Maybe," said Jo. "We saw all these people in blue sweatshirts here and wanted to know: What is this place?"

"It's a youth club," the boy answered. "Or … it was. The town hasn't got enough money for the club now. But Bob is 20 trying to save the place."

"Bob?" Jo asked.

"Yeah, Bob Stanley. He's our youth club leader. Do you want to go inside and meet him?"

"No thanks," said Dan and Jack.

25 "Sure," said Jo. "I'm Jo Shaw. And this is my friend Jack and my brother Dan."

"Hi," said the boys.

"I'm Harry," the boy smiled.

And the four of them went inside to meet Bob.

Chapter 6 Bob

....

Jack, Dan and Jo went into the old church with their new friend Harry. They were surprised: it didn't look like a church inside. It was like a sports centre!

They looked around. "Very cool, isn't it?" Harry said.

5 "Yeah," Jo said.

"Wow," said Dan and Jack.

"Bob?" Harry shouted. "It's me, Harry!"

"I'm here, Harry!" a voice called. The four boys went to where the man was. "Hi, Harry," he said. "Who are your

10 friends?"

"They asked about the club," Harry answered, "so I wanted to show them the place."

"Well," said Bob, "welcome to what was the St Paul's Youth Club. I'm Bob Stanley."

15 The boys said their names and shook hands with Bob. He was a young man, about 27 or 28. And he looked very strong.

"Our dad is a youth club leader," Dan said. "Maybe you know him – Mike Shaw?"

20 "He's got the club in Redcliffe, right?" Bob said. "His job is safe then."

"Yes, that's right," answered Jo. "But why do you say his job is safe?"

"Well, Redcliffe is a nice part of town. The new council is

25 only closing youth clubs in the not-so-nice parts."

"But that's stupid!" said Jack. "The kids in St Paul's need youth clubs too!"

"Of course they do," Bob said. "Youth clubs are important everywhere, but here in St Paul's they're really important."

"So why is the council closing this club?" Jo asked.

"Well," said Bob, "a lot of the parents here don't know how to complain. Some of them can't even speak English. Down in Redcliffe, lots of parents are teachers, doctors or
5 lawyers. The council doesn't want problems with them. That's why they closed this youth club last month."

"Last month?" said Jack. "But you're still here."

Bob laughed. "Well, I come for a few hours each week – Mondays and Thursdays. I don't get any money," he said.
10 "The council says we can stay till the end of the month, but we have to find the money to pay for the telephone and all the other little things."

Jack and Dan both wanted to ask a question: Where does the money come from? But they were afraid of the answer.

Jo asked their question for them: "Where do you get the money then?"

5 "I throw in a few pounds when I can," Bob said. "And some of the kids have summer jobs. They give some money when they can. And we sold the blue hoodies. We made lots of money from that. But now …"

It was very quiet in the old church. Then suddenly there 10 was a loud bleep.

"Sorry, a text message for me," Jack said. He took out his mobile and looked. "It's my mum. I have to go home."

The boys said goodbye to Harry and Bob. When they were far away from the old church, Dan said, "Are you two 15 thinking what I'm thinking?"

"That Bob is really nice?" asked Jo.

"No," said Dan, "that Bob is paying for the youth club with money from the corner shop robberies."

"I think you're right, Dan," said Jack. "The club, the 20 hoodies, they need money to stay open – it all fits. And there was another robbery today."

"How do you know?" Jo asked.

"Well," Jack said, "that message wasn't from my mum. It was from Sophie."

25 "Oh no! Not the Kapoors' shop!" said Dan.

"No, a different shop. Sophie heard about it on the radio. Let's go to Ananda's house and find out."

Chapter 7 Jack – a robber?

On Thursday it was Jack's turn to watch the Kapoors' shop.
It was boring work. At first he stood in front of Mr King's fish
shop. It was opposite the Kapoors' shop. But he didn't like
the smell of fish, so he went to a different place.

5 He was outside a travel agent's now. It didn't smell, and
there were lots of interesting posters in the window. But
the posters made him sad. Other people went to interesting
places like Spain, Greece, Turkey or Germany – or New York!
But he had to stay at home because his parents had a B & B.
10 He thought, "No more posters for me! And I can't watch the
shop and look at posters."

Jack sat down and took out his mobile. He had some
cool games on his mobile, and he started to play. But he was
careful: he always had one eye on the Kapoors' shop.

15 Jack was in the middle of a game of Football Pro Action
when he suddenly saw a man's legs next to him. "What are
you doing there, young man?" a voice said.

Jack was very scared, but he looked up. It was a policeman!
"I'm playing a game," Jack said.

20 "Why here, out on the street?" the policeman asked.
"I'm watching the corner shop over there," Jack said.
"Yes, I can see that," said the policeman. "That's why I'm
here."

"What do you mean?" Jack asked.
25 "Two shop owners called the police about you."
"About me?" Jack didn't understand. "Why?"
"Do you know about the Corner Shop Robbers?
"Yes," answered Jack. "That's why I'm here."
"So you're working for them?"

"Well, I'm not really working for them. I'm just helping them."

"Come with me, young man," the policeman said.

"Where are we going?" Jack asked.

5 "I'm taking you to the police station."

"But I can't go," Jack said. "I have to watch the shop. So I can call you if the robbers come."

"If the robbers come?" Now the policeman didn't understand. "But you said you're helping the robbers."

10 "No, no," said Jack. "I'm helping the Kapoors. It's their shop. I go to school with their daughter."

But the policeman just said, "Come with me, son."

"Please don't take me to the police station," Jack said. "I …"

15 "We aren't going to the police station," the policeman said. "We're going to the corner shop. Then we can check your story with Mr and Mrs Kapoor."

Jack and the policeman crossed the street and went to the Kapoors' corner shop.

20 "Hello," said Mrs Kapoor when the two went into the shop. "Hi, Jack."

"So you know this young man?" the policeman said.

"Yes, of course," answered Mrs Kapoor. "He's Jack Hanson, my daughter Ananda's friend. Is there a problem?"

25 "No, I don't think there's a problem," said the policeman. "We're trying to watch all the corner shops now – the robberies, you know."

"Yes," said Mrs Kapoor. "Thank you very much. Oh, would you like a cup of tea?"

30 Mrs Kapoor and the policeman talked and talked. Just then Jack saw three people outside. Three young men with blue sweatshirts! The three looked inside the shop, but

they didn't come in. Jack was sure it was the robbers! "And they didn't come in because they saw the policeman," he thought.

Jack went outside to see where the three young men went. But he was too late. They weren't there.

"Do I tell the policeman what I saw?" Jack thought. "No, I don't think so. Maybe it wasn't the Corner Shop Robbers."

But Jack knew – he knew: "The robbers want to rob the Kapoors' shop next!"

Chapter 8   The SHoCK Team makes plans

The next day, Jack told the SHoCK Team what he saw. Everybody was worried. But they were excited too.

"Maybe we can catch the robbers," Jo said.

"Yes, great," Ananda agreed, "but what about my
5 parents?" The group was in the Kapoors' kitchen, and Ananda pointed downstairs.

"The robbers aren't dangerous," Jack said. "I heard that on the radio."

"It was in my dad's newspaper too," Sophie said. "Don't
10 worry."

"But they have baseball bats," Ananda said. "They …"

"Wait, Ananda," Dan said. "They're talking about the Corner Shop Robbers on the radio."

"… the seventh robbery of a corner shop in Bristol this
15 summer," the man on the radio said. "There were no injuries in yesterday's robbery. But the robbers used their baseball bats to break bottles and a window. They were angry because the shop's owners didn't want to give them money. And now on to more news: Bristol City Council …"

20 Ananda turned off the radio. The friends were quiet for a minute. Then Jo said, "So, I can watch the shop on Monday. Who wants to work with me?"

"I do," everybody said, then laughed.

"Well, we can't all watch the shop," Sophie said.

25 "Then I suggest that some of us go to St Paul's," Dan said. "We can watch the blue hoodies and follow some of them."

"How do we know which ones to follow?" Jack asked.

"Well, we're looking for a group of three," said Dan. "Maybe one group looks suspicious."

"Sounds good to me," Jack said. "Ananda, why don't you come to St Paul's with Dan and me? Sophie and Jo can watch the shop."

"I don't know, Jack," Ananda answered. "I want to be here, near my parents."

"I'm sure it's OK, Ananda," Dan said. "Dilip can be here for your parents."

"That's a joke," Ananda said. "Dilip thinks these robberies are great."

"What?!" everyone said.

"Yes," said Ananda, "He's just happy that he doesn't have to work in the shop. He's out with his friends every day."

"I see," Sophie said. "But if there are problems, your parents don't want to have you here."

"But I want to help," Ananda said.

"You are helping, Ananda," Dan said. "Just not here."

"Oh, OK," Ananda said.

"Right, so Sophie's and my job is to watch the shop," said Jo, "and the three of you go to St Paul's and follow the suspects."

"Don't worry, Ananda," Sophie said. "With Jo and me here, nothing bad can happen."

Chapter 9   The SHoCK Team in action

....

On Monday afternoon, the SHoCK Team met at Jack's house.

"Has everybody got their mobiles?" Jack asked.

"Yes, we have," they all answered.

5   "Then let's synchronize watches," Jack said. "It's 3.36. OK?"

"OK!" answered the SHoCK Team.

"Good. Well, you all know what to do. Let's go."

Ananda, Dan and Jack got on their bikes to go to St Paul's.

10 Sophie and Jo started to walk to the Kapoors' shop. But before they left, Ananda said, "Sophie, Jo. Please watch my parents."

"Don't worry, Ananda," Sophie said.

"The SHoCK Team is there for them, Ananda," Jo said.

15 "Thanks, everybody," said Ananda. "I hope the police catch the robbers today. Dilip and I go to New York on Wednesday."

And with that, Ananda, Jack and Dan rode to St Paul's, and Sophie and Jo walked to the Kapoors' corner shop.

20 "I'm nervous," Sophie told Jo.

"Don't worry, Sophie," Jo said. "I'm here with you."

"Thanks Jo." But she was still worried.

They were very quiet till they got to the Kapoors' shop. Then Jo asked, "Where do you want to stand and watch?"

25 "How about over there," Sophie suggested, "in front of the travel agent's?"

"Good idea," said Jo. And they went there to watch.

It was 4.25. Dan, Jack and Ananda rode past the old church where the boys in blue hoodies met.

"Just a few more minutes," Jack said.

"Where do you want to wait?" Ananda asked.

5 "Let's stay on our bikes," Jack said. "We can ride up and down till we see a suspicious group."

"Good idea," said Dan.

Suddenly the door to the old church opened, and boys in blue hoodies came out: one big group at first, then lots of 10 small ones. Ananda rode past them, then Dan, then Jack. They met at the end of the street.

"I saw two groups of three," Ananda said.

"Me too," the boys said.

"I can follow one group," Dan said, "and you two can 15 follow the other one."

"OK," said Jack. "And remember: if you see anything suspicious, call us."

"Don't worry, Jack," said Dan. "I don't want to be a hero. Those boys looked big!"

20 It was 5 o'clock. Opposite the Kapoors' shop, Jo and Sophie waited.

"I'm hungry," Jo said.

"And I'm thirsty," said Sophie.

"Why don't I go to the Kapoors' shop and get some crisps 25 and lemonade?" Jo suggested.

"What about the robbers?" Sophie asked.

"It's too early for the robbers," Jo said. "No problem."

"OK, but I don't want lemonade," said Sophie. "I"d like some apple juice please."

30 "Right," said Jo. "Lemonade and crisps for me, apple juice for you."

"Yes, thanks, Jo."

Jo crossed the street to the Kapoors' shop. He went inside and said hello to Mr Kapoor.

"Hello, Dan," said Mr Kapoor. "How are you today?"

5 "I'm fine, thank you, Mr Kapoor," Jo answered. "But I'm not Dan – I'm Jo."

"Oh, I'm sorry," said Mr Kapoor. "I'm never sure who is Dan and who is Jo."

"That's OK, Mr Kapoor. A lot of people have that problem."
10 Jo started to look for his crisps. "Er, Mr Kapoor? I can't see any cheese crisps. Have you got any?"

"Yes, we have," Mr Kapoor answered. "Behind you, on the bottom shelf."

"Oh, I see them," Jo said. "Thank you, Mr Kapoor." And he bent down to get them.

Suddenly Jo heard voices: "This is a robbery." "Give us
5 yer money, old man!" "We don't want to hurt you. Get into the back room."

Jo stayed on the floor and listened. "I hope Sophie saw them come in," Jo thought. "And I hope they don't find me here."

10 On the other side of the street Sophie tried to watch Jo cross the street and go inside the Kapoors' shop. Suddenly she heard a voice. "Well, hello Sophie."

She knew that voice. It was Miss White, her music teacher. "Hello, Miss White. Er, what are you doing here?"

15 "I live near here," Miss White said. "I just wanted to do some shopping. And what about you?"

"Er, I'm just looking at the posters here at the travel agent's."

Sophie and Miss White talked for a few minutes. Sophie tried to watch the shop most of the time. But she didn't see
20 the three boys in blue hoodies go inside.

Jack and Ananda followed a group of three boys from the youth club in St Paul's. The boys walked around a lot. Then they went into a corner shop.

25 "This is it," Jack said. "Is your mobile ready?"

"I'm ready. 9 – 9 – 9, then …"

"Wait!" Jack shouted.

Ananda looked up. The boys with the hoodies were now back on the street. Each had a lemonade or a cola in his hand. And they weren't in a hurry.

"I don't think they're our robbers," Jack said.

5 "No, they aren't," said Ananda. "Do you still want to follow them?"

"Not really," Jack answered. "Why don't I call Dan and see what his group is doing?"

Dan walked with his bike for a few minutes and followed
10 his group. And then they got on a bus. "They're in a hurry today," he thought. And he followed the bus on his bike.

Now the bus was at a red light, and Dan was behind it on his bike. Suddenly his mobile rang. He saw the number and knew it was Jack. "Maybe it's important," he thought, and
15 so he answered his phone.

Dan watched the bus leave, but he had to answer the phone. "Hi Jack. What's happening?"

"Ananda and I are sure the boys in our group aren't the robbers. Do you need help?"

20 "No, I'm still following them," Dan answered. "They're on a bus."

"A bus?" Jack said. "But then the times are all wrong! I hope they're not the robbers."

"Me too," Dan said. "Look Jack, I have to go. I don't want
25 to lose them."

"Right," said Jack. "And why don't I call Jo and tell him the robbers are early – if they are the robbers!"

The light was red again, so Dan had to wait. But that was OK: he knew the bus and where it went. "When the light is
30 green, I can still find the bus," he thought.

When the light was green, Dan rode off. He found the bus in a few minutes and followed it again. But then he thought: "Oh no! Maybe they got off the bus when I was on the phone."

5   Dan rode up next to the bus and looked inside. There were only five people on the bus – and there were no boys in blue hoodies! "Why did Jack have to call then?" he thought. Then he rode back to the bus stop where the boys in hoodies got off.

10 He looked around, but he didn't see the blue hoodies. "Where are they?" he thought. Then he realized: the Kapoors' shop wasn't far from where he was! "Oh no!" he thought. And he got back on his bike and rode to Ananda's house.

Chapter 10 The robbery

....

Jo was still on the floor of the Kapoors' shop, behind a shelf. The robbers didn't know he was there. "Where are the police?" he thought. Then his mobile rang.

"What was that?" one of the robbers said.

5 Then Jo heard somebody behind him. "It was a little kid with a mobile," the young man said. Then to Jo: "Give me that."

Jo gave him his mobile.

"Now get in the back room with the old man," the robber
10 said. Jo did what the robber told him and went to Mr Kapoor. When he was inside, he heard the robber lock the door.

"Are you OK, Jo?" asked Mr Kapoor.

"Yes, I am," Jo answered. "And you?"

"Don't worry about me," Mr Kapoor said. "I'm fine."

15 "Sophie is watching the shop, Mr Kapoor. She knows to call the police if the robbers come."

Sophie waited and waited for Jo, but he didn't come out of the shop. She was worried. "Maybe the robbers came when Miss White was here, and I didn't see them," she thought.
20 "I know. I can cross the street and look inside the shop from the outside. And if something is wrong, I can still call the police."

Sophie crossed the street and went to the window of the Kapoors' shop. "I can't see anything," she thought. "Maybe
25 if I go over there, where there's no sun."

She started to move, but then she heard another voice: "Come inside, kid." She turned and looked. It was a young man in a blue hoodie. And now she was their prisoner!

The young man pushed Sophie into the shop and took her mobile. Then he opened the back room and pushed her inside. She was surprised to see Jo and Mr Kapoor in there. When the robber closed the door again, Jo whispered, "Did
5 you call the police?"

"No, I didn't," Sophie whispered back. "I didn't know the robbers were here."

"Oh no," said Jo. "We can't stop the robbers now. I'm sorry, Mr Kapoor."

10 "Don't worry," Mr Kapoor answered. "It's only money, Jo. We're all OK, and that's the important thing."

Dan rode very fast, and when he got to the Kapoors' shop, he didn't see Sophie or his brother. He was worried. "Maybe they went inside the shop," he thought. So he went inside too.

5   When he got inside, he knew it was a mistake. Three boys with blue hoodies were there. They had big sports bags, and they already had all the cigarettes from the shop and lots of alcohol in the bags. The boys looked up from their work. They looked surprised.

10   "Hey," one of them said.

"How …" another one said.

"What …" said the third.

Dan tried to run, but the boys were too fast. They caught him.

15   "How did you get out of the back room?" one boy asked.

Dan didn't understand. "The back room?" he thought. Then he realized: "They've got Jo in the back room. And they think I'm Jo!"

20   He was very scared, but he tried to sound strong. "It was easy," he said. "There's a door to the outside in the back room. So I left and called the police."

The boys with the hoodies looked nervous. "Let's go before the police get here," one of them said.

25   They started to leave, but then one of the other robbers said, "Wait a minute. I don't believe you, kid. Why did you come back then?"

"Er, … ah, I didn't think you were still here," Dan answered.

30   "Come on, Neil," said one of the robbers. "We've got what we wanted. Let's go."

The robbers ran out of the shop and disappeared down the street. Dan then went to the back room and opened it. Jo and Sophie were the first to come out, then Mr Kapoor. He went to the phone and called 999. "Police please," he said.

5   Suddenly there was a noise at the door. All of them looked – they were afraid it was the robbers again. But it was Jack and Ananda.

"We saw three boys with blue hoodies run out of the shop!" Jack shouted. "They went right on Weston Street."

10   Ananda ran to her dad. "Are you OK, Dad?" she asked.

"Yes, I'm fine," Mr Kapoor said. "I'm just happy your mother wasn't here."

"Well, the SHoCK Team didn't do a very good job this time," Jo said. "We can't help the police now."

15   "Don't be so sure, Detective Jo Shaw," said Sophie. "I have an idea."

Chapter 11   Sophie's idea

The police came to the shop only two minutes after Mr
Kapoor's phone call. They were happy: "The robbers can't
be very far away," one of the policemen said. "You got out
of the back room and called us only a few seconds after they
5 left."

"Do you think you can catch them then?" Mr Kapoor
asked.

"Well, I've got four cars out there," the policeman said.
"They're all looking."

10   Then Dan went to the policeman and said, "We want to
help."

"Not now," the man said. "This isn't for kids."

"But I think I know who they are," Dan said.

The policeman looked at Dan. "You do?"

15   "Yes, I think so," Dan answered. "They go to St Paul's
Youth Club. And one of their names is Neil."

"And I know how you can catch them," said Sophie.

"How, young lady?" the man asked.

"Well," Sophie said, "the robbers took Jo's and my
20 mobiles. And both mobiles are on."

"And?" the man asked.

"And I saw on TV that the police can find where a mobile
phone is when it's on."

"That's brilliant, Sophie!" said Dan.

25   "Well, we can try. Why don't you give your mobile
numbers to that policewoman?" he said and pointed to a
policewoman. "Then she can call the mobile company. I
want these robbers too, you know!"

Police catch Corner Shop Robbers

Group of schoolkids helped

Corner shop owners in Bristol can now sleep at night: the police arrested the Corner Shop Robbers yesterday after their eighth robbery.

The robbers were three young men, 17 and 18, all from Bristol. All three went to St Paul's Youth Club. The club's leader, Mr Robert Stanley, was shocked when he heard that three of "his" boys were the Corner Shop Robbers.

"They're good kids," Mr Stanley said. "I think they were bored. There's nothing for kids to do here. The club is only open for a few hours each week. The council hasn't got enough money. And they're closing the club at the end of the month."

When the police told this newspaper about the arrests yesterday, there were five very clever young people there. These five students from Cotham High School helped the police to find the robbers.

The five, twins Dave and Jo Shaw, Jack Hanson, Sophie Carter-Brown and Ananda Kapoor, say they are the "SHoCK Team". These teenage detectives watched the corner shop of Ananda Kapoor's parents and waited for the robbers. When the robbers came, they called the police.

Mr Ravi Kapoor, the owner of the shop, said, "I'm very proud of my daughter and her friends."

Mayor wants more money for youth clubs

Mayor Bradshaw asked Bristol City Council yesterday for more money for youth clubs. "I want to open St Paul's Youth Club again," the mayor said.

"Great article, isn't it?" Jo said. The SHoCK Team was in the Kapoors' kitchen.

"They got my name wrong," said Dan.

"Yes," said Sophie, "why did they think it was Dave?"

5   "Reporters get things wrong all the time," said Jo.

Dan looked at his brother. "Hey, didn't you talk to the reporter, Jo?"

"Me?" asked Jo. "Maybe a little."

"Jo," said Dan. "Did you tell her my name was Dave?"

10   "Why do you think that, little brother?" Jo said.

"Because you …"

"Wait!" shouted Jack. "There's something about us on the radio."

"… helped the police to arrest the Corner Shop Robbers. The five, Dan and Jerry Shaw, Jack Hanson, Sophie Carter-Brown and Ananda Kapoor, are students at Cotham School in Bristol. And now the weather."

5   Ananda turned off the radio. Everybody laughed – but not Jo.

"Jerry Shaw?" Jo said. "How did that happen?"

"Like you said, Jo," said Dan, "reporters get things wrong all the time."

Vocabulary

A

a few [fjuː] ein paar
alcohol ['ælkəhɒl] *hier:*
  alkoholische Getränke
angry ['æŋgri] böse, verärgert
answer: (to) ~ the phone ans
  Telefon gehen
around: (to) walk ~ [ə'raʊnd]
  herumlaufen
(to) arrest [ə'rest] festnehmen
arrest [ə'rest] Festnahme
at first [ət 'fɜːst] zuerst, anfangs

B

baseball bat ['beɪsbɔːl
  ˌbæt] Baseballschläger
behind [bɪ'haɪnd] hinter
(to) believe [bɪ'liːv] glauben
(to) bend down [bend] sich
  bücken
bent [bent] Vergangenheitsform
  von „bend"
bleep [bliːp] Piepton
bored: She was ~. [bɔːd] Ihr
  war langweilig.
born: (to) be ~ [bɔːn] geboren
  werden/sein
bottom shelf ['bɒtəm] unterstes
  Regal
brilliant ['brɪliənt] brillant, genial

C

careful: Be ~. ['keəfl] Seid
  vorsichtig. / Passt auf euch
  auf.

(to) catch [kætʃ] fangen,
  schnappen
caught [kɔːt] Vergangenheitsform von „catch"
centimetre ['sentɪmiːtə]
  Zentimeter
cigarette [ˌsɪgə'ret] Zigarette
(to) clap [klæp] (Beifall)
  klatschen
company ['kʌmpəni] Firma,
  Gesellschaft
compass ['kʌmpəs] Zirkel
(to) complain [kəm'pleɪn] sich
  beschweren
council ['kaʊnsl] Gemeinderat
(to) cross [krɒs] überqueren
cup of tea [ˌkʌp_əv 'tiː] Tasse Tee

D

dangerous ['deɪndʒərəs]
  gefährlich
doctor ['dɒktə] Arzt, Ärztin
(to) draw [drɔː] zeichnen
drew [druː] Vergangenheitsform von „draw"

E

everybody ['evribɒdi] jeder, alle;
  ihr alle
excited [ɪk'saɪtɪd] aufgeregt,
  freudig erregt
(to) explain [ɪk'spleɪn] erklären

F

fast [fɑːst] schnell
(to) fight [faɪt] (be)kämpfen

G

(to) get bekommen
   (to) get holen
   (to) get sth. wrong sich (bei
   etwas) irren, etwas falsch
   machen
got [gɒt] Vergangenheitsform
   von „get"
go-kart ['gəʊ kɑːt] Gokart
(to) guess [ges] (er)raten
guess [ges] Vermutung

H

(to) hear [hɪə] hören
   heard [hɜːd] Vergangenheitsform von „hear"
hoodie ['hʊdi] Kapuzen-
   Sweatshirt
(to) hope [həʊp] hoffen

I

if wenn, falls
important [ɪmˈpɔːtnt] wichtig
injury [ˈɪndʒəri] Verletzung

K

Korean [kəˈriən] koreanisch,
   Koreaner/in

L

lawyer [ˈlɔːjə] Anwalt, Anwältin
leader [ˈliːdə] Leiter/in
light: red ~ [laɪt] rote Ampel
(to) lock [lɒk] abschließen
(to) look for suchen

(to) lose [luːz] verlieren
loser [ˈluːzə] Verlierer/in

M

map [mæp] Stadtplan
(to) mark [mɑːk] markieren,
   kennzeichnen
mark [mɑːk] Markierung
mayor [meə] Bürgermeister/in
(to) mean [miːn] meinen
meeting [ˈmiːtɪŋ] Versammlung
mile [maɪl] Meile (etwa 1,6 km)
(to) miss [mɪs] vermissen

N

news (no pl) [njuːz] Nachrichten
nothing [ˈnʌθɪŋ] nichts

O

on: (to) be ~ an sein,
   eingeschaltet sein
opposite [ˈɒpəzɪt] gegenüber
   (von)
owner [ˈəʊnə] Besitzer/in

P

past sth. [pɑːst] an etwas vorbei,
   an etwas vorüber
pattern [ˈpætn] (Tat-)Muster
(to) pay for sth., [peɪ] etwas
   bezahlen; etwas finanzieren
(to) plan to do sth.
   vorhaben, etwas zu tun
police station [pəˈliːs steɪʃn]
   Polizeirevier
policeman [pəˈliːsmən] Polizist
prisoner [ˈprɪznə] Gefangene(r)

(be) proud of sb./sth. [praʊd]
    stolz auf

R

rain [reɪn] Regen
rainy ['reɪni] verregnet
(to) **read** [riːd] lesen
    read [red] Vergangen-
    heitsform von „read"
(to) **realize** ['riːəlaɪz] sich einer
    Sache bewusst werden
reporter [rɪ'pɔːtə] Reporter/in
(to) **ring** [rɪŋ] klingeln
    rang [ræŋ] Vergangenheits-
    form von „ring"
(to) **rob** [rɒb] überfallen,
    ausrauben
robbery ['rɒbəri] Raubüberfall
(to) **ride a bike** [raɪd] Rad fahren
rode [rəʊd] Vergangenheitsform
    von „ride"
round: ~ **the corner** [raʊnd]
    um die Ecke

S

sad [sæd] traurig
safe [seɪf] sicher
(to) **save** [seɪv] retten
second ['sekənd] Sekunde
(to) **shake hands** [ʃeɪk]
    sich die Hand geben
    shook [ʃʊk] Vergangen-
    heitsform von „shake"
shocked [ʃɒkt] schockiert
(to) **smell** [smel] riechen
smell [smel] Geruch
(to) **speak** [spiːk] sprechen
(to) **stay away (from)**
    fernbleiben (von)

strong [strɒŋ] stark
stupid ['stjuːpɪd] dumm
sun [sʌn] Sonne
surprised [sə'praɪzd] überrascht
suspect ['sʌspekt]
    Verdächtige(r)
suspicious [sə'spɪʃəs] verdächtig
(to) **synchronize watches**
    ['sɪŋkrənaɪz] Uhren
    gleichstellen

T

teenage ['tiːneɪdʒ] Jugend-,
    jugendliche(r, s)
text message ['tekst ˌmesɪdʒ]
    SMS
travel agent's ['trævl ˌeɪdʒənts]
    Reisebüro
Trial and Error [ˌtraɪəl ˌənd ˈerə]
    Versuch und Irrtum
(to) **turn around** [ˌtɜːn ə'raʊnd]
    sich umdrehen

V

victim ['vɪktɪm] Opfer
(to) **visit** ['vɪzɪt] besuchen

W

weather ['weðə] Wetter
What's wrong? Was ist los?
(to) **write** [raɪt] schreiben
    wrote [rəʊt] Vergangen-
    heitsform von „write"

Y

youth club ['juːθ klʌb]
    Jugendclub, -zentrum

Names

Alexandra Road
[ˌælɪgzɑːndrə ˈrəʊd]
Alma Road [ˌælmə ˈrəʊd]
Ananda Kapoor
[əˌnændə kəˈpɔː, kəˈpʊə]
Bob Stanley [ˌbɒb ˈstænli]
Chaplin Road [ˌtʃæplɪn ˈrəʊd]
Cliff Whittaker [ˌklɪf ˈwɪtəkə]
Cornwall [ˈkɔːnwɔːl]
Cotham [ˈkɒtəm]
Dan Shaw [ˌdæn ˈʃɔː]
Emily [ˈeməli]
Germany [ˈdʒɜːməni]
Greece [griːs]
Harry [ˈhæri]
Jack Hanson [ˌdʒæk ˈhænsn]
Jo Shaw [ˌdʒəʊ ˈʃɔː]
Majorca [məˈjɔːkə]

Mayor Bradshaw [ˌmeə ˈbrædʃɔː]
Meera [ˈmɪərə]
Miss White [ˌmɪs ˈwaɪt]
Mr Kingsley [ˌmɪstə ˈkɪŋzli]
Mrs Khan [ˌmɪsɪz ˈkɑːn]
Neil [niːl]
New York [ˌnjuː ˈjɔːk]
Pak Lee [ˌpɑːk ˈliː]
Prunella [pruˈnelə]
Ravi [ˈrɑːvi]
Redcliffe [ˈredklɪf]
Sophie Carter-Brown
[ˌsəʊfi ˌkɑːtə ˈbraʊn]
Spain [speɪn]
St Paul's [sənt ˈpɔːlz]
Turkey [ˈtɜːki]
Walton Street [ˈwɔːltən striːt]

Check your understanding

....

After you read a chapter, try to answer the questions about it. If you know the answers, then go to the next chapter. If you don't know the answers, you can look at the chapter again.

Chapter 1
1) Who is in the SHoCK Team?
2) What plans have the kids in the SHoCK Team got for the summer?

Chapter 2
1) Why does Jo miss school?
2) Why doesn't Sophie want to call her friends? And why doesn't Ananda want to call her friends?

Chapter 3
1) Why are the Kapoors worried when they find out about the robberies?
2) What do Ananda and her mum find out at the meeting?
3) Why does Ananda think of the SHoCK Team?

Chapter 4
1) What does the SHoCK Team plan to do at first?
2) What does the Team find out about the robberies with a little 'detective work'?

Chapter 5
1) Where do the boys in hoodies come from?

Chapter 6

1) Why does Bristol Council want to close the St Paul's youth club, but not the club in Redcliffe?
2) What do Jack and Dan think about Bob Stanley and the robberies?

Chapter 7

1) Why does the policeman talk to Jack?
2) Why does the policeman take Jack to the Kapoors' shop?
3) Why does Jack think the robbers want to rob the Kapoors' shop next?

Chapter 8

1) What do the SHoCK Team hear on the radio?
2) What are the Team's plans for Monday?

Chapter 9

1) Why can't Dan stay with Jack and Ananda?
2) Where is Jo when the robbers come?
3) Why doesn't Sophie see the robbers?
4) What does Jack mean when he says, 'the times are all wrong'?
5) How and where does Dan lose 'his' group of blue hoodies?

Chapter 10

1) How do the robbers find Jo? And Sophie?
2) Why are the robbers surprised when they see Dan?
3) What do Jack and Ananda see when they get to the shop?

Chapter 11

1) What do Dan and Sophie tell the police?

Chapter 12

1) Why does Mr Stanley think that the boys robbed the corner shops?
2) Why was Dan's name wrong in the paper? And why was Jo's name wrong on the radio?